Old Delhi - Where elephants go to school!

AIRMAIL FROM...

OLD DELHI - WHERE ELEPHANTS go to school!

Michael Cox

Illustrated by
Rhian Nest James

Hippo

Scholastic Children's Books,
Commonwealth House, 1-19 New Oxford Street
London WC1A 1NU, UK

A division of Scholastic Ltd
London ~ New York ~ Toronto ~ Sydney ~ Auckland
Mexico City ~ New Delhi ~ Hong Kong

Published in the UK by Scholastic Ltd, 2000

Text copyright © Michael Cox, 2000
Illustrations copyright © Rhian Nest James, 2000

ISBN 0 439 01273 2

Old Delhi – where elephants go to school! is part of a series of books about fascinating countries around the world. Each book is made up of letters written by a boy or girl who lives in one of these countries. You might find that their English isn't always quite right (unlike yours, which is always perfect – ha ha!). So watch out for a few mistakes and crossings out. Sometimes in their letters the children use words from their own language (just like we all do!).

Hari, who writes these letters, occasionally uses words from the Hindi language. Like "namaskar" which means "hello". Don't worry! You already use quite a few words that came from India in the first place. Like "pyjamas". . . and "bungalow", and lots, lots more. So a few new ones shouldn't be too hard, should they?

28 November

Dear letter-wallah,

Namaskar (hello). Good morning. How are you? My name is Hari Sharma and I am living in the big city called Delhi, which is in India. I have just come to live in this busy huge place. At the moment I have got hardly any friends. All my old ones are behind in my village. But do not cry for me. I will make some new ones soon. No problem! I am a happy, friendly and nattery person. But, in the mean time, do you mind if I am being <u>your</u> pen friend? I will write to

you and tell you all about what it is like to be me and about India too. And some other gossipy things! You will not regret this great decision. So, here we are going. . .

WHOOOOOSH

7

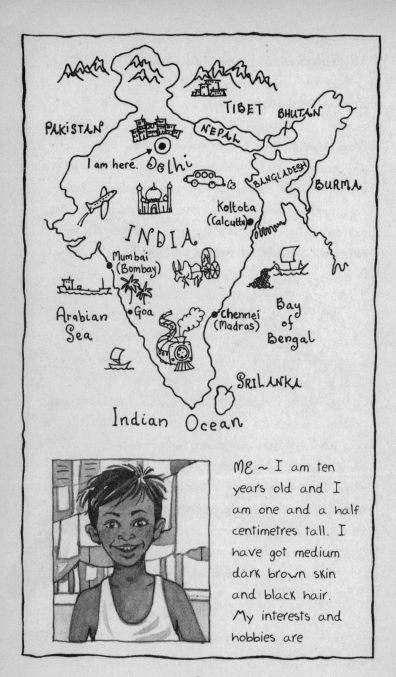

TIBET
BHUTAN
PAKISTAN
NEPAL
I am here. Delhi
BANGLADESH
BURMA
Koltota
(Calcutta)
INDIA
Mumbai
(Bombay)
Arabian
Sea
Goa
Chennei
(Madras)
Bay
of
Bengal
SRILANKA
Indian Ocean

ME ~ I am ten years old and I am one and a half centimetres tall. I have got medium dark brown skin and black hair. My interests and hobbies are drawing, bicycling, cricketing and writing. But not all at the same time! (Arf arf arf! - that's me laughing - you will get used to it.) Also, I am a lunatic about reading. I often have my head buried in a book.

FAMILY~ I have got one sister called Pushpa. She is 19 and next year she is going to be married. But we do not know who to. My mum and dad are looking for the right boy for her. This is how most weddings happen in India. Your parents choose who is going to be your partner for your life.

I will let you know when they find her one.

I have also got one brother called Hari who is five. Yes, that is right! We are <u>both</u> Hari! I am Hari One! And he is Hari Two! Because he is the youngest. Sometimes also my dad and mum are calling us Big Hari and Little Hari.

My mum is called Laxmi and she looks after the family. Prempal, my dad, is a top expert car and motorbike fixer. He was the best Mr fix-it-wallah* in our village - he was also the <u>only</u> Mr

9

fix-it-wallah in our village! (Arf arf arf!) Here
we all are:

Some weeks ago my uncle Darshan wrote this
note to Dad (he is not really my uncle - in India
you can call a really good friend "brother" or
"sister" and Darshan is Dad's oldest friend):

Prempal my brother. Delhi car-mending
business expanding like wildfire. Need
top spanner man quick sharp. Yes! You!
Bring all family too! Soon as possible...
I will give you BIG money. No sweating!

So, here we are! We came on a train that was four hours long. Tomorrow my bapuji (daddy) is going to start his new job at Darshan's Car Hospital No Job Too Big. He is very chuffed. He says that now we will have

more money than ever before. If I am good he will buy me a <u>new</u> bicycle. (My old one is all clapped in.)

For the moment we are living with Uncle Darshan and Aunty Meena and their five children in their flat. It has got only two bedrooms so we are squashed. Especially as we have brought our daada (grand-daddy) with us. I was forgetting to tell you about him! His name

daada ↘

is Jatinder and he is very old with false teeth and whiskers.

Soon we will be moving to our own place. Good! Then I can escape from uncle Darshan's children. They are

sometimes being horrible to me for no reason at all. But no matter. I am being very tough when I am wanting to.

mr tough guy Hari One

Right this moment I am hiding from them so I can write this first letter to <u>you</u>. Uh oh! I think I can hear them coming now. So I will sign off quick. I look forward to corresponding with you at my nearest conveniences.

Here they come, the horrible ones! I am gone!

Bye bye!

Hari

Last quicky!
* A wallah is our Indian word for a person or a job-doer. So now <u>I</u> am <u>your</u> airmail-wallah (arf arf!).

18 December

Hello good morning reader-wallah,

Namaste (greetings). How are you? Here is the news from your special India correspondent, Hari Sharma. By the way, I am one and a half <u>metres</u> tall. Not one and a half centimetres, like I told you!

FIRST NEWS! At last we are in our own place. Hoorah! In our village we lived in a mud and dung and thatching house with fields all around it. It had only two rooms with soil on the floors. Mum and Pushpa did nearly all our cooking outside on a fire made from cow poos. We had no electricities and had to fetch our water from the well which was quite a big walk away!

Our new house here in Old Delhi is not like that at all! It is made from cement and bricks and tiles and breeze blocks. It has three rooms with electricities and a water tap quite handy just around the corner. Also a nice verandah for doing cooking. We are snug as a rug in a bug! We are renting it from Mr Singh. He has got a whole building full of them.

The dhobi wallah (laundry)

water tank

pigeon loft

Mum cooking

Our neighbour, Deepak

Our verandah

food and cloth shops

People queuing for water

SECOND NEWS! Dad is happy with his new work. He says he is rushed off his fingers doing mending at Darshan's Car Hospital No Job Too Big. Soon we will get a pile of money! (New bicycle here I come!) Yesterday I took his tiffin (lunch) to him there.

It was quite an adventure, I can tell you, old chum! Mum gave me daddyji's tiffin carrier and the directions but I was being so busy staring at fantastic sights that I was suddenly lost! As I was wondering where to turn next I saw some boys run to a car parked right by me and tear off the screen wipers.

Then they hopped in an alley and were gone! Next moment a man ran to me and grabbed my neck scruff very hard. He said, "Hey you. Your friends just stole my wipers and you were their lookout. I'm going to call a cop. You will be going to prison for this!" Pen-chum, I was <u>deeply</u> afraid!

But then another man came and said "No! This boy was not with them! I saw the thieves with my very own eyes. They ran off to the car-parts bazaar!" And I thought, "<u>That</u> is the place I want to go!"

When I got there, guess who was talking to my dad? The boys with the wipers! They were trying to sell them to him so I whispered to his ear what had happened and he wagged his finger on them and said, "You bad bad bad boys. Take those vipers back this minute or

I will box your ears for you!" And they ran away.

After I had shared my dad's tiffin with him I walked home through the alleys and lanes. My eyes were jumping this way and that. So much to see! And my nose was full to bursting. So much to smell! And my ears were being clobbered by a thousand noises. Shouting, hooting, mooing, roaring! What a din! All around me there were busy busy people doing their going and coming. Look, I have drawn it for you on the next page. I am sorry. I cannot give you the smells. Please make them up in your nose.

I am still not completely happy about living in Delhi but after today I am thinking it is a very <u>interesting</u> place to be.

<u>Important information</u> (do not eggnore!) - If we are sticking "ji" on the end of your name it is meaning we have great respect and love for you!

Hello penpalji!

Your airmail-wallah,

Hari

Street Life

We have lots of people for building jobs. These very poor people come to Delhi from their villages to earn money for food.

Horns painted the colours of the Indian flag

Cartload of spices

Sikh Shop keeper

A heavy load!

Beggars

A boy having his teeth pulled by the dentist wallah.

Man having his beard cut.

What a funny hairstyle this man has!

11 January

Namaskar readerji!

How are you today? I am feeling very rosy.
Here is why! Today my daddyji came home with
a great big pile of books for me. A second-hand
junk shop man gave them to him for doing a
lovely car-mending job for him!

Wow, penji! You should see them! They are
mainly in English and quite old. Some are maybe
even leftovers from the days when British people
were in charge here more than 50 years ago. There
is everything! The Guide to English ~~Grandmas~~
Grammar, The History of India, guides and maps
of Delhi, The English of Dictionaries!

Today I have been reading a book about Delhi. And I have found out that it is really <u>two</u> cities. They are called New Delhi and Old Delhi. Old Delhi (where our flat is) has been here for hundreds and hundreds of years. But New Delhi was only built here by the British from 1911! In 1912 they made it the capital city of India. Our old capital was Calcutta. Right this moment (and just a bicycle-ride away from where <u>I</u> am now living!) the top-job wallahs of the Indian goverment are making big and important decisions for our country! Well, here is <u>my</u> secret, pen chumji! One day <u>I</u> would like to be one of those very top-job wallahs too. But of course, I will only get that if I tune up my brains with lots of reading and studying!

Now, talking of books and learning, you are probably wondering about my school. Well, for the moment I do not go. I was at one in my old village for part of the time but since we have come to Delhi I haven't got one.

My old school

Yes, I know! You are now feeling <u>very</u> sorry for me because I am not a really <u>lucky</u> child like <u>you</u> and cannot go to school every day just like you do!* All over India there are children like me. Some do not go to school <u>ever</u>! They just work in factories or farms from when they are very little until they are old. But that will <u>not</u> be me! I will get myself a new school here later or sooner. But at the moment, I have to make some rupees for my family. So I am doing that, this and the others. Running errands for our neighbours, doing queuing for them . . . and suchlike jobs.

Do not worry though. While I am waiting for my new school I will polish my brain knowledge up with my new old books.

Also in the second-handy shop my daddyji saw a . . . <u>bicycle</u>! Not brand new and also needing some repair jobs. But still quite lovely. He says he will buy it for me <u>very</u> soon! Hurrah!

And now for some more brain polishing with my new books.

Goodbye chumji!

Hari

* I think I am maybe quite jealous of you!

17 January

Namaste palji!

Good morning. Hari Number One here! What are
you like today? Here in Delhi I am very busy.
As well as being number one local errand boy I
have got important new position. I am also now
number one finding-it-fetching-
it-carrying-it-polishing-
it-cleaning-it-
tinkering-it-making-
cups-of-chai*-
answering-the-
telephone-wallah
at Darshan's Car
Hospital No Job Too
Big.

   In my spare moments I am reading my books.
I have learned
dollops! My teacher is
very pleased with me.
Because he is ME!!
(Arf arf arf arf arf!)
   Yesterday I was
looking at my map
book. Did you know that India is the seventh
biggest country in the whole world?! Our shape is

like a big triangle and we are as large as all Europe put together, but without Russia. Look!

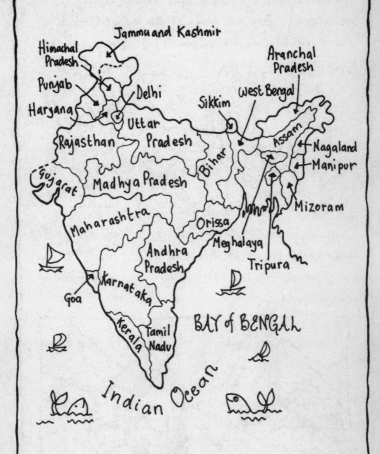

Aren't we a whopper! This famous little Indian story will show you how <u>different</u> all over India is. Some blind men wanted to find out what an elephant was like. One put his hands on its trunk and said, "Ah! It is like a snake." Another felt its body and said, "No, it is like a wall!" Another touched its tusk and said, "Wrong! It is like a pole!" Another grabbed its leg and said, "No it isn't, it is like a pillar!"

India is like that elephant in the old story. It is different things to different people here. If you ask a person in the north what India is like they will tell you. . .

India is high mountains with snow and hard rocks.

In the middle someone will tell you. . .

If they are in north west they will say. . .

In the south or the coast they will tell you. . .

India is a tropical jungle with great rain and coconut palms.

My pen-palji! India is <u>all</u> of these things and many, many more. But! One thing that you will find the same in many places is that India has crowdfuls of people. After China we are the most bursting-with-humans country in the whole world. We are <u>brimful</u>! We have got almost one billion and are getting more every day.

Just since starting this letter to you nearly <u>2,000</u> new Indian babies have been born! Even here in Delhi, our capital city, there are 10 million people!

That is how many live in the whole country of Belgium!

I have got to go errand-dashing into these

crowds of Delhi-wallahs in just a few minutes. But before I do I will put on my big pully-over. Right now it is cold in Delhi. (We are not hot all the time.) The other day I even saw some goats in their woollies! Their owner had put them in old cardigans so that they would not be frozen to their bones!

Now I must go to the car parts bazaar for Deepak, our neighbour. Someone has swipered the wipers from his taxi!

Phir milenge (goodbye).

Your best pen-pal,

Hari

* our word for tea

27 January

Good morning pen-friendji!

How are you? Hari here with some more news
for you. Yesterday our whole family had a day-
out treat. We went to New Delhi! Wow, penji!
What a smart place it is! All full of tip-top
buildings with many VIPs (very important people)
and money-bags wallahs living there. All very
different from where _we_ live in Old Delhi.

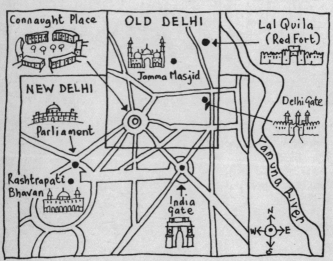

We went there because it was Republic Day. This is the day we celebrate India getting free from the British who were ruling us until 1947. What a fantastic time we had. When we got there huge crowdings of people were lining the Rajpath. That's the wide big road which goes from our President's Palace to the huge big arch called India Gate. A flame is always burning there to remember all our Indian war heroes.

Suddenly there was a huge roar in the sky and I looked up at the most thumping great helicopter you ever did see. It gave Little Hari a big fright and he began to cry! Next moment this clattering great flying machine began to <u>bomb</u> us! Not with explosion bombs! But with <u>flower petals</u>. Soon a monsoon of colours was raining down on top of us.

And then the great parade was on! Chumji, there were thousands of smart soldiers and

sailors and army top-brass wallahs all stamping
past us. And soldiers riding on trotting horses,
spitting camels and plodding elephants. As they
streamed past our Prime Minister and his
important friends they gave him smart salutes.

There were also dancers and music bands and
moving platforms on wheels showing everyday
things from all the different parts of India.
Everyone was crazy with excitement and cheering!
I waved my India flag until I thought my

shoulders would fall off! I felt as proud as punch for my great nation!

Penji, please try to come and see our Republic Day parade. It is the biggest in the whole world, you know! But, if you do, <u>do not</u> bring your bag or your camera. They will be taken away from you by the police! It is for security. They are worried that someone will try to kill our PM (Prime Minister) or one of our top VIPs with a gun or bomb. It has already happened before to our famous PM, Mrs Gandhi and later on to her PM son, Rajiv.

Best hopings,

Hariji

PS Uncle Darshan and Auntie Meena's eldest boy, Vishal, came with us to the big parade. Maybe it will be him who marries my sister. I hope so. He is a very nice and kind boy. Not a bit like his crazy younger brothers and sisters!

1 February

Dear penji,

Hariji scribbles-wallah here! Howdah you do?
Since we went to the big parade I have had
elephants on my brain. Of all the great sights of
that smashing day they were my most favourite.
I have gone mad on these great beasts and I
have been swotting them all week! I have written
you a special elephant guide. So please enjoy it.

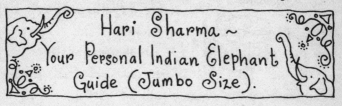

Hari Sharma ~ Your Personal Indian Elephant Guide (Jumbo Size).

Indian elephants are smaller than African ones
and in India only the man elephants have tusks.
Elephants are all over the place here. Yesterday I
even saw one sitting on top of neighbour Deepak's
taxi!

Jewellery

Models →

Statues →

clothes

buildings

sweetie tins

Many are jewellery and model ones. Others are made from wood or stone on buildings and temples. Some are decorations on clothes like on my mum's sari. And on the sweetie tin that my grand-daddy keeps his false teeth in. Maybe <u>all</u> Indian people have got elephants on their brain?

In the jungles there are real wild ones. Long ago people thought they would be useful so they caught them with ropes and tamed them. They trained some to be war elephants who would carry soldiers and fight other ones.

Others were made into work elephants. Nowadays they do work like getting log woods from the forest, giving rides to tourists and carrying the bridegroom at rich people's weddings. My daddyji says they are even more useful than a truck. He has never ever had to mend one!

The men who drive them and teach them are called mahouts. When an elephant is a baby lots of mahouts stroke it many, many times. This will get it used to them and show it that they are all being its chums.

A mahout and his elephant are special friends. They will work together for many, many years. When it is five years old the elephant goes to school to learn all the things it must do. It can understand many words - but does not speak them. (Arf arf!)

After seven years of learning the elephant is ready to work. For being good and working hard the mahout gives the elephant a bath in the river every day. (That is _more_ than I get!) Sometimes he rubs coconut shells on its body because the elephant likes that.

Here is a mahout story my grand-daddy told me. A boy mahout was in the jungle with his teacher mahout and an elephant. In the night a tiger came to their camp and ate his teacher. Even after eating a whole mahout, the tiger was still hungry and wanted to eat him too! But when the tiger came to eat the boy, his elephant picked him up with its trunk and put him under its own front legs. It kept him safe there all night long until the tiger went away. I would like an elephant best friend. How about you?

There are still 6,000 wild elephants in India. Some bad men kill them and take their tusks and head parts for ivory. The ivory is made into ornaments. Sometimes into little ivory <u>elephants</u>! But what is the point of that? It is much, much better to have all our elephants alive and happy and full of beans! By the way, did you know that if an elephant's tusks are cut off low down (the part below the inside nerve) it is not being a problem at all to them. The tusk grows back again, just like your finger nail after cutting!

Sometimes wild elephants flip their lids and go very crazy! Some came to a village where grand-daddy's uncle was living and drank all the beer from the brewing store. Then they charged about and squashed all the houses. And even two people as well! Altogether 400 people are killed by elephants in India every year. But I think that Indian cars and trucks kill many more!

I have got to go now . . . I am in a big hurry. This evening my daddyji brought home my new old bicycle from the second hand junk shop. We are going to start mending it!

Hari

PS Today a boy I have never seen before came to call for Pushpa. I do not think I like him too much. He called me "titch" and twisted my ear. Maybe she will marry _him_? I hope not.

18 February

Namaskar my computer-brains pal,

How are you? Here in India it is Holi. This is our spring festival time when people go fruity as nut cakes with parties and running around throwing coloured water on each other. It is to celebrate the coming back of our warm weathers! Today I was greened and pinked all over by a boys' gang with water pistols! I didn't mind. I was laughing a lot.

In between having Holi fun and doing my part-times jobs I am still being my own teacher. And giving myself lots of smacks when I am not paying attentions! (Arf arf!)

Last week grand-daddy and me were talking about old times India. He told me of some good (and some <u>very</u> bad!) things that happened here and then I read some more in my books. Today I am going to tell you a bit of this story. Not all though. That would take me for ever and always! I have done it in bits and pieces. Some today and a bit more in some other letters.

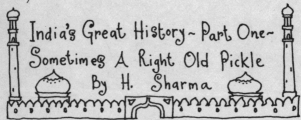

India's Great History ~ Part One ~ Sometimes A Right Old Pickle By H. Sharma

THE VERY VERY OLDEN DAYS ~

India has been here a very, very long time but it has not always been called this name. There were people living here many thousands of years ago. Some began the Hindu religion here and ruled the roost.

THE NOT QUITE SO OLDEN DAYS ~

In the sixteenth century Muslim-religion people
from the middle part of Asia came here and
did fighting with the Hindu-religion people. They
grabbed some of India for part of their big
empire. It was called the Mughal Empire and
was here for more than 300 years.

The Mughal Empire was very important for
India and you can see leftover forts and
palaces and other great buildings from it all
over the place. It had lots of emperors. I
cannot tell you about them all but here are
three of the most famousest and interesting ones:

AKBAR THE GREAT ~

Akbar became emperor in 1556 - when he was only <u>12</u> years old! He was quite kind and understanding to people who were not Muslims (such as Hindus) and asked them to help him rule. This was a good idea because it meant there was no falling out between people of different religions

and his empire stayed peaceful and cheerful. While Akbar was in charge lots of great buildings and gardens were made in India. He even had a whole beautiful new city built. It was called Fatehpur Sikri.

After only 14 years Akbar and all the people left the amazing city because they could not get water. It is still there but now an empty ghost place! Akbar died in 1605. (But not of thirst. Arf arf!)

SHAH JAHAN ~

Shah Jahan was Akbar's grandson. He was in charge from 1627 to 1658. Shah Jahan's wife died after she had had their 14th baby. He was so very, very, very upset that he got 20,000 of his men to build a huge tomb to keep her body in. It took them 22 years! It is one of the most famous, most beautiful buildings in the world. It is called the Taj Mahal. Have you heard of it?

Two other great things that Shah Jahan had built were the Agra Fort and the Red Fort. The Red Fort is here in Old Delhi quite near to where I live.

In 1658 Shah Jahan's third eldest son, Aurangzeb, killed his two big brothers and then put his daddy in prison inside Agra Fort and took over being emperor. Shah Jahan spent the rest of his life looking out of his prison window at the Taj Mahal and feeling very sad.

AURANGZEB ~

Aurangzeb was a different kind of ruler than his daddy and his great grand-daddy had been. He was not understanding of other religions and did bad things like knocking down Hindu temples and making people pay money taxes to have religions that were  not Muslim. Because of this there was much rebelling and fighting in India. After Aurangzeb died in 1707 the big Mughal empire began to fall to pieces. A hundred years later it was on its very last legs. And this gave the British their chance to completely take us over. I'll tell you how they did that in my next India history story!

Best wishes and phir milenge,

Hari Number One

PS We have nearly finished mending my new old bicycle. It is almost ready for the road!

1 March

Hello to you old thing,

Today I have been for my first
ride on my new old bicycle. My
dear chumji, I am wishing I had
not! I have come home all of a tremble! It was
very scary indeed!

To ride your bicycle anywhere in India you
have to be brave. But I think to do it right here
in Old Delhi you must have to be completely
mad! The traffic is CRAZY. There are many,
many sorts and they do not care for you one bit!
They will squidge you flat as a chapati* and
not even bat their eyes. We are supposed to go
on the left like in the UK, Australia and Japan.
But I think this is a joke. Everyone is all over
the road. And all the time they are honking
honking honking.

My dad says Indian drivers think their horn
is most important bit of car. They will bring their
cars to him with baldy tyres, broken brakes and
falling-off wheels, then say, "Fix horn please. Yes
just horn!" So it is biggest-noisiest wins. And
every bicycle for himself! All the time I was
swerving this way and this to save my skins.
Also some bad boys drove their bicycles straight

48

into me and chased me. By the time I got home
I wished I was back at my village. At least
<u>there</u> I might have enjoyed my ride!

My good pen-pal! Sometimes I think I will never _ever_ get properly used to being in big, busy, noisy Delhi. It is so, _so_ different from where I used to be. I will tell you about my old village, then perhaps you will see what I mean. This is what it was like!

For a start-off the houses and buildings and stuff did not go on for ever and ever and ever like they do here. There was just a nice bunch of about thirty dung and thatching houses with a little road (not at all busy!) going to the fields where we grew our food. Yes! All nice and peaceful.

In the middle of all the houses was a big space where the market was held for people to do their buyings and sellings. My auntie Kerpal had a stall there where she sold mangoes and water melons. Sometimes she gave me one for nothing! Next to Auntie's stall was a banyan tree where people like to sit in the shade and have a chat with their pals.**

Our village was a friendly place and everyone knew everyone else. I don't think I will get to know all the people in Delhi if I live here five lakh years!*** Near to the market place was the big water pool we called the tank. It was a big favourite with me and all my pals. On scorching hot days we would have lots of fun throwing ourselves in and out!

And then, best of all, palji, there was my old school (which I am missing <u>a lot</u>!). It was just one room and we had to sit on the soil floor because there were no tables and chairs. But we all absolutely <u>loved</u> it. Because we had Mr Chatterjee! The nicest, cleverest, kindest teacher in the world!

The teacher was the number-two most important person in the whole village. (I suppose it is just the same in your village.) But of course, the number one most important person was our priest.

There was always something happening in our village. But not in

the crazy-mad-rush-you-push-you way it does in Delhi. In the mornings my mum did our washing at the stream with all the other mums while Dad went off to his workshop. At lunchtime she carried Dad's tiffin to him while some other mums took tiffin to the people who were working in the rice fields. Rice is very important for Indian villages. Both for selling and for eating. More than 500 million people eat rice every day in India, you know. Sometimes I helped with the rice harvest picking. It was very hard work and hurt my back.

As well as the farm workers, our village had a weaver to make our clothes, a pot-maker to make dishes and a carpenter who made wooden furniture things like baby cots and stools. There was also a cobbler who made and mended shoes. And, of course, there was Mr fix-it-wallah, my daddyji! So we had everything we needed. Daada said the village was just the same when he was little and probably for hundreds of years before that too! Mr Chatterjee said it is much the same all over India with four out of every five people living in villages very much like our one.

For our entertainments we had festivals with Indian music and dancing. Also, in the market place, we had a television that the government had given to the village. In the evenings people would watch it. Most of the programmes were <u>really</u> boring. The big <u>proper</u> treat for everyone was to visit the film cinema in the nearby town to see the brilliant movie, then all talk of it non-stop on the bus home.

So that is a bit about my old life! Now maybe you can see why sometimes I feel so homesick. Even though my daddy is getting such big moneys here in Delhi. I sometimes think I will run away back there. Maybe on my bicycle?

...or maybe not!

I will stop now or I will be getting tear splashes on your letter. But not really! (Arf arf!) To tell you the truth, I am feeling OK again now that I have told you all this.

So thank you for listening.

Hariji

* This is our bread - it is flat (Arf arf!).
** Did you know that in the Indian city of Calcutta we have got the biggest banyan tree in the world? It is 240 years old and its branches spread so far out that it measures 420 metres around the outside!
*** A "lakh" is our word for 100,000.

5 April

Dear fruity tooty!

How are you, my pal? Are you working your stockings off for your teacher? I bet you are! Here in Old Delhi things are not looking too good in the Pushpa-marrying department. The Ear Puller has been back <u>again</u>! He had tiffin with us today and was <u>very</u> polite to my mum and dad. They seem to like him a <u>lot</u>! It is looking like he might be the one for my sister. And no sign of Vishal <u>at all</u>! Poor old him. And poor old <u>me</u>!

Achaa! (OK!) Now to other stuff! Yesterday I was looking at my big India map and my old grand-daddy was looking over my shoulder. (He is wild to be learning too.) He put his ancient finger on my map of India and said, "Listen,

Hariji! When I was very little a long time ago I thought India was just a tiny, tiny, small place and Britain was a . . . GREAT BIG one! Because in the old days British people came across the world

56

and put us in <u>their</u> empire. Like a giant spider putting a little fly in its web. Then I saw the map and knew it was the other way around. <u>We</u> are the GIANT and <u>they</u> are the tiny one! Ha ha ha, Hari! How surprised I was!"

My grand-daddy is right. Look, here is India next to Britain.

But now you are probably thinking, "However could they do it?" For part two of my India history me and Daada have made you this picture story to show you how this amazing thing happened.

16TH CENTURY~ Some European people began to come here to nosey around and do trading.

1600 ~ In England the Queen of Elizabeth I made some of her men into the East India Company.

NEXT 200 YEARS AND MORE~ The British kept coming here and doing lots of buying and selling. This made them rich and powerful. They even had their own army with Indian soldiers in it! And more and more Indian people for servants.

END OF 18TH CENTURY~ The big Mughal empire was really falling to pieces by now. And the British got even <u>more</u> power in India.

BEGINNING OF 19TH CENTURY~ The British were bossying nearly all of India about. And they played a clever (and <u>naughty</u>!) trick on the Indian people. This was it: they took all the best natural things from here and sent to Britain.

Back there - in rich men's factories - their <u>own</u> poor people made them into things.

Then the things came back to India and the Indian people had to buy them back again!

No wonder the rulers and bosses all got so fat and rich!

1857~ The British rulers upset their Indian soldiers by putting dead cow grease on the bullets for their guns. Killing cows is against the Hindu religion, and so the British were forcing the soldiers to go against their own beliefs.

So there was a mutiny by the Indian soldiers and a punch-up with the English all over the place.

Eventually the British got back on top.

1878 ~ So we hardly had finished being in one empire before we got plonked in another!

The British being in charge of India was called the Raj (our word for rule). But to find out how we got back in charge of ourselves watch out for the last part of my India history. Coming soon to a letter-box near you.

Hari Number One

16 May

Dear mail-wallah,

Namaste! How do you do? Today I am happy
Hari! Because of great news! In some months'
time Pushpa's wedding is going to happen. She <u>is</u>
going to be married! And not to horrible Mr Ear-
Twister after all. But to good old Vishal!

Hurrah! Mum and Dad have sorted
it all out with Uncle Darshan and
Auntie Meena. We are are all very
pleased for Pushpa. She is very
lucky to be getting a really
nice boy like Vishal and we are all
looking forward to the great
celebrations. I will keep you
posted.

Now to <u>my</u> capers. As usual I am
errand-dashing all over the place!

Today, when I was going to the shop to buy
some ghee* for my mamaji, I saw a crazy crowd
on the pavement ahead of me. "Oh no!" I

63

thought. "Some sort of a terrible trouble is taking place!" As I got closer I saw it was all nothing to worry about! Just a very big crowd of excited men standing outside an electrical shop. They were watching the cricket match on the TV in the window!

It was India against England. And India were winning! (Hoorah!) So I stopped to watch for a bit. I don't know how long I was there, but suddenly I remembered the ghee! Now it was

my turn to be on a sticky wicket! It was two whole hours later when I got home. Then it was two tight slaps for poor Big Hari! (Little Hari thought that was very funny!)

After my slaps I went out into the street.
Guess what! A gang of kids were playing cricket
in the lanes. And the biggest one said, "Do you
want to play, kid?" So I did. And now I have
made some really good friends here in Delhi!

Another sport that Indians are world-tops at
is hockey. We have won Olympics medals for it.
And we also have polo. This exciting game is like
hockey but you play it on horses. The people who
live in Kashmir first thought of it but the British
rulers got very keen for it too. So they took it for
themselves! Of course! You don't always have to
do polo on horses. You can use. . .

. . .camels,

. . .elephants,

. . .your friends,

. . .or even your bicycle.

It is very good fun. I would like to play bicycle polo, but <u>not</u> in the Delhi traffic!

Do you play chess, chumji? And do you know who invented it? We did! Yes, chess is an Indian game. Maybe when we meet I can beat you at our game? (Arf arf!) Howzat!

Hari

* ghee is a sort of butter we use for cooking

2 June

Dear western-wallah friend,

How are you penji? Have you had your corn flops yet?

Remember how I was telling you about the mix-up of people-varieties we have here in India? Well, all these different sorts of people speak their own different sorts of languages. Because there is <u>NO</u> such language as <u>Indian</u>.

The people I am seeing in the streets are speaking all sorts of languages. The policeman who waves at the traffic near the car-parts bazaar is from the Punjab. So he is speaking Punjabi.

The shoe mender who I am sometimes doing nippings around for is from Bengal. So he is speaking Bengali.

Deepak, our taxi-wallah neighbour, is from Kashmir. So he is speaking Kashmiri.

As well, they are all speaking Hindi too. And _that_ is what I am speaking! It is my number one language. It is the official language of India. This means the government would like _everyone_ to speak it. But everybody doesn't want to!

Altogether in India we have got 23 main languages and hundreds and hundreds of little ones. On our rupee Indian-money notes the writing is done in 13 of our big languages so everyone here can know what it says. Look! I will do you some writing in Hindi so that you can see what it looks like. I bet that you cannot guess what this means:

यह गाय है।

No? Well! That is how we write our word for "cow" - our most special animal!

MOO!

Now then, here's a surprise for you! More people in India speak English than in <u>England</u>! We are the second biggest English-speaking country in the world. America has first place, I think! Remember the British were in charge of India for a long time? So here is one thing they left for us, instead of just taking away! English is very useful for us, even though not <u>everybody</u> by a long way speaks it.

Indian businessmen, judges and top rulers use English to write and speak much of the time. The writing on our stamps and money is in English as well as Hindi. Knowing English is also very useful and handy for Indian people who go to live and work in other countries. Do you know some Indian people? And, of course, it is handy for writing to you, pen palji!

Now! Here's your surprise number two. You are maybe speaking some Indian language without even knowing it! All the time the British rulers were busy-bossying Indians about they were using our words. And they took some back to England with them. Soon people back in England were talking with Indian words. Look at my list and see how many of our words you have pinched from us. Then give them back to me immediately! (Arf arf!)

pyjamas

Bungalow

Jodphurs

bangle

Juggernaut

dinghy

dungarees

verandah

thug

bazaar

candy

ghouls

Shampoo

It's not just these few, there are <u>thousands</u> more! Ask your teacher if they know them! OK, to finish you with - because you are my best pen-friend - I am going to give you some more Indian words <u>completely free of charge</u>. They are my Hindi ones.

How are you? — Aap Kaise hain?

OK — Acha

Good bye — Phir milenge

Thank you — Dhan yavad

My name is Hari — Meera naam Hari hai

If you have Indian friends perhaps you could give them a surprise and try these out on them? But make sure that they are speaking Hindi first!

Anyway, bye bye! Phir milenge!

Hariji

23 June

Dear letterji,

Namaskar. Hello to you and good night. How are you being? Here it is our hot summer season and we are being sizzled at 45°C. At night we are sleeping on our roof for coolness. Lucky it is a flat roof - not sloping!

The hotness makes smogs from the traffic that goes in your mouth and up your nostrils. It is most uncomfortable! As well as all that our water tap is running dry. But forget the heat and listen! Something most interesting has happened this afternoon. I was lying on my bed having a nice cool wafting from my fan and a bird flew in my room and crashed with the fan.

It fell on my bed. I thought, "It must be dead!" But I was wrong. I carried it to my mamaji who was cooking a chicken on the verandah. But she said, "Nothing we can do, Hariji. We are not a vet."

Sizzle, sizzle!

Then Deepak taxi-wallah walked past and I showed him the bird. "No problems, Hariji!" he chirped. "We can take him to the Delhi Bird Hospital." And we raced away in Deepak's taxi with the bird in a crudboard box.

Do you have a bird hospital where you are? The one in Delhi is quite famous and is at the Digambara temple. It is

looked after by people called the Jains. They try to care for every living creature in the whole world. It is their religion. That is why they never eat meat and look after hurt birds and help make them well again. Some of the Jain people wear a mask over their mouth because they don't want to hurt any creature. It is to make sure that they don't even swallow a tiny insect by mistake! Have <u>you</u> ever swallowed a fly? I did once. They don't taste so good, do they?

mask

Jain Nun

At the hospital they took the bird from us and said they would make it better. You do not have to pay but Deepak put some rupees in their charity box to help them. While we were there we saw all sorts of birds. Sick pigeons, partridges who had been shot by hunters, hens which had been knocked down by rickshaws and even some hurt squirrels too.

On the roof there were big cages with the birds who were almost better and ready to fly away. Sometimes the Jain carers cannot make the birds better so they die. When this happens they burn their bodies and say prayers for them at a special ceremony on the Yamuna River (the main one that flows through Delhi).

On the way home through the market place we

saw lots of birds for sale in cages. They looked very down in their ~~mouths~~ beaks. I think they would like it much better at the bird hospital!

Have you got birds where you live? Big and busy Delhi is absolutely flapping with them. They are everywhere. Five hundred different sorts altogether! On our flat block roof is a bird that

can speak three languages: Hindi, English and Punjabi! It is a myna and it is our neighbour's pet. It swears too!

So that was that! Yes! I'll be jiggered, penji! Fancy them having a hospital here

that is just for birds. What a good thing! Especially if you are a badly battered bird!

Phir milenge.

From your pen pal,

Hariji

12 July

Dear friendji,

How are your doings? Here in Old Delhi great sheetings of rain are gushing from the sky and the streets are being flooded. It is our monsoon season, the time when it rains and rains for more than two whole months. Do you have one? When the first monsoon rains came in my old village Mr Chatterjee always used to shut our very leaky school for the day. Then we would all run outside and make paper boats from our exercise book pages and float them in the floodings. It was great fun. (Arf arf!)

Because of all the wets I am not Delhi-dashing so much. Today I have stayed indoors and used my brain-power to do the very last part of the India history for you. It is about a tremendous man who helped get India free from Britain. Read it! It is a great story!

India History - Part Three - The Story of Mahatma Gandhi and How We Got Our Country Back for Ourselves.

By the time it was the early twentieth century many Indian people were fed up to their front teeth with the British treading on them. Me too (if I'd been alive!).

A brave Indian man called Mahatma Gandhi decided it was time to do something.

He said that Indian people should let the British know they did not like them being such bossy boots and should refuse to do their work.

This caused all sorts of problems. In one place, called Amritsar, a British General made his soldiers shoot at Indian people who were having a protest meeting. They killed nearly <u>400</u> of them and wounded <u>1200</u> others!

This <u>terrible</u> thing made all Indian people very angry and upset. Gandhi said that India should still try to get rid of the British peacefully, but by other ways. Here are two of the things he did to show the Indian people what he meant:

1. He stopped wearing clothes that had been made in Britain and wore traditional Indian cotton cloth ones which he had made for himself.

I want to wear Indian clothes that have been made in India!

2. He marched to the seaside and boiled some seawater to make salt then pretended to sell it a bit at a time.

Why should we have to buy our own salt back from the British?

The British did not like this at all because they had put themselves in charge of <u>all</u> the salt-making and selling in India. But the Indian people loved it and soon got the idea of <u>not</u> doing what the British wanted.

We refuse to buy our own things! We want to be in charge of our own country!

By now the British were fed up to <u>their</u> front teeth with <u>Gandhi</u>, so they put him and 100,000 of his supporters in prison! But he was a top

Indian hero and millions and millions of people all over India loved him to bits. The British knew they could not put <u>all</u> of them in prison. It was a BIG problem for them. They knew they could not keep squashing India. So in the end they set Gandhi and his friends free. Then in 1947 they gave India its independence to be in charge of itself and went home.

Sadly, there was still trouble to come. Some of the new India leaders were Hindu-religion people and some were Muslim-religion people. They could not agree about the way the new India should be. They argued.

In the end the Hindus had the main part of India to live in. Pakistan was broken off for

Muslim people. This was called Partition. Muslims left India to go to Pakistan and Hindu people left Pakistan to go and live in India.

There was terrible fighting between the Muslims and Hindus as they forced each other from their homes. Thousands were killed. It was a very bad time. Gandhi was very upset by it and said to the Hindus,

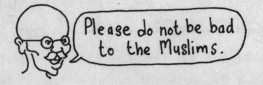

Some Hindus were very angry with Gandhi for saying this so they made a plan to kill this great man and shot him dead completely! This terrible, terrible happening made everyone in India so very upset that most of the fighting stopped.

Since then Pakistan has been Pakistan and India has been India. There are still some Muslim people in India and some Hindu people in Pakistan. Sometimes there is still falling out. India is a democracy, which means that every one can have a vote to say who will be in charge. We are the biggest one in the whole world!

So there it is, our India history almost right up to today! Now I am going off to Darshan's Car Hospital. My daddy is going to show me how to give a car a fresh drink of oil and water. It is part of my new training to be . . . Top Car Mender No Job Too Big! (Arf arf!)

I'll pen you again when I get a jiffy to spare!

Best wishes,

Hari

30 August

Dear chumji,

Me and Little Hari and daddyji are here on our
own in Old Delhi this week. Daada, Mamaji and
Pushpa have all gone to Varanasi. That is our
holy city on the river Ganga (Ganges). The water
in the Ganga river is special. People who have the
Hindu religion (like my family) go to Varanasi to
bathe in it and drink it. We believe it will wash
away our badness and give us new life. All
Hindu people try to do this at least one time in
their life. It is called a pilgrimage. My daddy
has paid for the trip with some of his job money
from the car hospital. When he told my old
grand-daddy he would
do this he became
delighted and got
teardrips in his eyes. He
has never been to
Varanasi and may
never get a chance again
because he is so ancient.
   Now! What religion
are you? And how
many gods have you got? Just the one? Or
thousands, like me? Or maybe you are thinking

that your religion is not important? No matter! I will tell you about <u>our</u> religion! Being close together in our families and having our religion is <u>very</u>, <u>very</u> important to all Indian people. It makes us all feel comfortable and happy. Everywhere you go in India you will see places for all the different sorts of religions. There are stupas for Buddhist people. . .

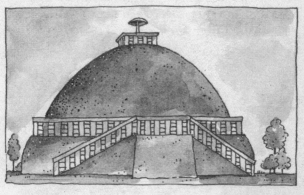

. . .mosques for Muslim people. . .

. . .churches for Christian people. . .

. . .gurdwaras for Sikh people. . .

. . .and temples for Hindu people.

THE HINDU RELIGION

My family are Hindus. It is the biggest religion in India. About three-quarters of our people believe in it. Here are some things about it. . .

1. WHAT HINDU PEOPLE BELIEVE~

We believe we are born and then we die. And then we are born again. Maybe we come back better than we were before. Or maybe worse. If we do good things in our life we will come back to a better position. But if we do bad we will come back worse. So it is important for us to do good things. Simple, isn't it? This trying to

be better is called helping our Karma. We pray to our gods for their help to be good. If we always come back as something better in the end we will get to <u>moksha</u>. This means we

will stop being born and dying and everything will be just perfect.

2. WHERE WE WORSHIP ~
Hindu people do their puja (worship) in temples called mandirs and also in their homes. In our flat we have got a special place for praying. It has a picture and some little statues and pictures of Ganesh. (More about him in a tickle!) We burn incense there too. The smell is very nice.

3. AN IMPORTANT RULE ~
Many Hindu people believe you should not kill animals. So a lot of them don't eat meat, though some do (like

my family). But <u>no</u> Hindu people ever eat beef.
For Hindus, cows are all very, very special. That
is why they can do whatever they want. If one
lies down to sleep in the road we have to wait!
They are very special <u>and</u> useful. They pull
ploughs and carts (and lawnmowers!), they turn
well wheels, they give dung for fires and building
and to make soil fertile. And they give us milk!
What a wonderful animal they are!

pulling plows and carts

What nice cows!

milk

dung

4. OUR HINDU GODS ~ There are thousands,
so I will just tell you these few, the first three
being the most important:

Brahma is the brilliant Creator god. He made all things. He has got four heads and four arms. The other gods have got lots of temples but Brahma has only got one.

Vishnu is the Preserver god. He looks after things. He has also got four arms but he has got blue skin too! He holds a big shell, a throwing discus, and a lotus flower.

Shiva is the fierce Destroyer god. He has got a third eye in his forehead! He carries a three-spiked fork called a

trident and rides on a big
bull who is called Nandi.

Kali is the frightening
goddess of destruction. She
has a necklace which is
made of skulls! She can
give you disease and
unhappiness, but she can
also make you better if she
feels like it.

Parvati is really beautiful
and she is Shiva's wife.

Ganesh is my favourite god
(and my family's). He
overcomes problems. He has
got an elephant head.
Now I will tell you how
he got it.

Ganesh was one of Shiva and Parvati's sons.
Shiva came back from a very long journey and
saw a young man guarding Parvati when she
was in the bath.

He thought she was being the man's girlfriend so
he lost his temper and cut off the man's head.
But the man was Ganesh! He had grown up and
changed quite a lot while Shiva had been away.
Shiva did not recognize him. Shiva
was very upset about cutting off
his own son's head. The only
way he could bring Ganesh back
to life was to give him the head
of the first creature he saw.
This was an elephant. That is
why Ganesh has an elephant's head!

I suppose that maybe you are now thinking you would like to be Hindu. Well, I am sorry. I have to tell you that if you are not born a Hindu you cannot be a Hindu. You will just have to carry on being you and keep the religion that you have got now!

I would like to tell you all about the other Indian religions too, but I have not got space. Maybe some other time?

Hari

PS Pushpa says she will send me a letter from Varanasi. I have asked her to send <u>you</u> one too. So watch your step!

3 September

Dear pen-pal of Big Hari,

Namaste. Greetings to you. I hope you are
feeling good! I am Pushpa, Hari Number One's
big sister. I am writing to you from holy city of
Varanasi. Mamaji, Daada and me have
arrived here. At last! We came here on the
train from Delhi. It took more than 14 hours!
All very tiring.

   Hari thought it would be good for you to
know about Varanasi. It is a wonderful and
very old place. People have been living here for
more than 3,000 years. That is longer than in

any other city in the world! It is also a very <u>special</u> place. There are 2,000 temples here. Their tops rise into the sky and look very beautiful indeed.

This morning we all went to the Ganga Ma (Mother Ganges). Hindu people believe that this great river was made when a huge wild water crashed from heaven right into our god Shiva's hair. He made the fierce water behave itself and it became the lovely Ganges that goes all the way from the Himalaya mountains to the sea at Calcutta.

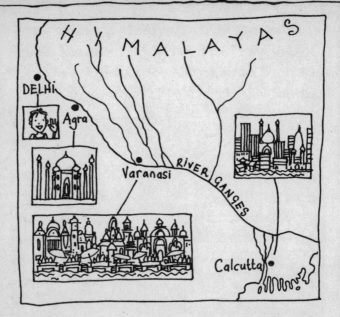

Just as the sun was rising we walked down the ghats (the steps at the sides of the Ganges) and into the water.

Then we threw our yellow marigold flowers on to the water. They were our presents for Shiva. Afterwards we washed ourselves with the holy river-water and Mamaji filled a little brass pot with it. Later on, when we were in the temple, she poured it on a Shiva statue. We believe that this makes sick people better.

After we had done our bathing we climbed back on to the ghats. They were crowded with

hundreds of Hindu pilgrims just like us. Also there were some sadhus making themselves ready for their day by brushing their teeths with twigs. Sadhus are Hindu holy men who wander around thinking about nothing but religion. They have long beards and hair and dress in yellow robes and carry a big stick and a begging bowl. Many of them rub fire-ash on their faces and bodies and some don't wear any clothes at all.

While all these things were going on boatloads of tourists were floating by and taking photographs of the ghats. I think they must have been very thrilled when two of the sadhus started to have a wrestling match!

Now I must tell you something which you may not like too much. Some of the ghats are for burning bodies. This is a special way for Hindu people to go away when they are dead. Many choose the ghats for being burned because a long time ago our goddess Parvati dropped her earring in the water here, so the ghats are very special. People bring the bodies of their dead family relatives here. They are wrapped in white cloth and carried on a green bamboo stretcher. Sometimes on the roof of a taxi if they have to come a bit further. They put them on piles of firewood on the ghat, then burn them and throw their ashes in the river. Also, Hindus believe that if you die at Varanasi you will get straight to Moksha and not have to keep being reborn. I think Daada would like this!

Now to something more cheerful! The last thing we did today was buy some Varanasi silk for me. The silk from here is very special and Indian girls like their wedding sari to be made from it. It is also very expensive! Just as it was getting dark we went to the place where the weavers were doing their work. Everywhere there was beautiful silk hanging on clothes-lines to dry after it had been dyed. The colours glowed like the feathers of a peacock.

Silk being woven into a sari.

We had a cup of tea with a silk-seller, then we bought my sari from him. It is a lovely pink colour with gold patterns on it. I love it and cannot stop stroking it.

   It has been a long day and I am tired so I will sign off now. It has been nice talking to you. I hope you enjoy the rest of Hariji's letters to you.

Yours faithfully,

Pushpa

PS I would really like you to come to my wedding but I think that maybe it is a bit far away.

20 October

Dear readerji,

Hello. It's me again, your old pal Hari Number One. How are you going along? Here in Old Delhi the ready-gettings for Pushpa's marriage to Vishal are growing bigger as each day goes by. And Pushpa is becoming full of excitement. Especially about her wedding sari! It is not just her who is having new clothes. We are all getting them!

As well as wearing her special silk sari and lovely jewelleries for her wedding, Pushpa will have her hands decorated with mehendi. This is a paste made from crushed up leaves from henna bushes and water and lime juice and oil. Mum will put it on Pushpa's hands the night before the wedding. The hand-decorating is a special ceremony that Indian people have been doing since 5,000 years ago. And just to make it last a good long time, my mum will put some tea into her mehendi mixturing too! It sticks much better with that!

mehendi ↓

Pushpa will also have some shindur powder put in the parting of her hair to show that she is married. The mehendi and the shindur powder are part of our wedding traditions. Another one will be for Vishal's mum and dad (Darshan and Meena) to break a fresh coconut on their doorstep when his new wife goes in their flat for the first time!

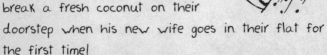

shindur

Have you ever seen Indian people in their traditional clothes? I have drawn you some of my friends and family in· theirs. Now you will know something about our dressings:

choli   pallav

Pushpa's sari is cloth material about one metre wide and between five to nine metres long (nearly the height of our flat block!). She winds it around her body and does not use pins or buttons to fasten it. She tosses the pallav (the last dangly part) over her shoulder. The short tight blouse she wears under her sari is called her choli.

This is daddy in his kurta and his churidhars - he likes to wear these when he is having his leisures - they are comfortable . . . and very <u>cool</u>! This is important for when we get our big hot weather.

Mrs Deepak taxi-wallah in her salwars - they are loose trousers like pyjamas that ladies from Punjab and Kashmir wear.

Her kameez is the long, loose top thing she wears with her salwars.

Kameez

Salwars

This is the lady from the flat next door in her burkha - this is a very big dress that some Muslim women wear so that all of them is covered up. Look - only her eyes are peeping out!

burkha

Deepak taxi-wallah wears a smart Europeans-type suiting and shirting. (Important to be smart for car-dashing in New Delhi!)

Mamaji says: "Plenty of room to grow, Hari!"

new suit

new trainers.

This is me! In my smart suit and my new trainers! Very nice, eh?

There are lots more, but I haven't got time to tell you them. I am dashing to the Car Hospital for my next training job. It's brakes-mending today!

Phir milenge,

Hari Fetch-And-Carry-No-Time-To-Spare!

17 November

Dear chumji,

Namaste! How are you? We are celebrating Diwali here in India at the moment. It is the special Hindu festival of light that we have just before our winter comes. We give our houses a big clean and light candles and exchange presents of sweeties. Everyone has great big bonfire parties with fireworks and thunderings and whoooooshings and sparklings everywhere! Have you seen Diwali celebrations in your country?

As well as Diwali, of course, my family are getting ready for our big event. So today we have been shop-tripping for Pushpa's wedding things. Chumji, I am very tired! We have thousands of small shopping places here but no enormous soup markets like I think you visit in Europe and USA. Here are some of the ones we have been to.

The first shop we went to was best!! Because it was the Ghantewala (Bell Ringer) sweet shop.

Grand-daddy says it is called that because in the old days there was a royal elephant who

The Elephant with a sweet tusk.

was sweets mad. Every time it passed this shop it stopped to ring the outside bell with its trunk until it got some sweeties. Then it would go away! Me and little Hari are like that elephant - sweety mad! Here are some things that Mamaji bought at Ghantewala. They are _all_ my flavourites!

Jalebis - orange-coloured tubes made from treacles all drippy with syrups.

Barfi - it is a fudge made from milk which has been boiled stiff.

Gulab jamun - fresh cheese soaked in rose syrup.

Kulfi - sort of Indian ice cream with spice and nuts.

(If you have an Indian sweetie shop nearby, try some!)

A lot of our sweeties have silver on them. Yes, it is _real_! It has been hit until it is as thin as thin can be, so you can _eat_ it! It is called vark. You can put it in all sorts of food. But do not touch it. It is so nearly not there at all that it will fall straight to pieces if you do! Mamaji has bought some silver leaves for going on the wedding food.

After sweety buying we went to Kinari Bazar (Braid Shop Street).

Kinari Bazar is an alley with many shops selling weddings things. We bought tinsels for decorating our flat and some rupee-note garlands. It brings good luck-fortune to give money at weddings.

After that Mum bought a big jar of pickle. Look who had to carry it home!

Then we tried some beards on. Little Hari asked if he could have one to wear at the wedding. (Arf arf!)

Shopping is thirsty work so we stopped at the water-seller wallah. He has the water in that goatskin bag on his back. We gave him some pice (little moneys) and he gave us a squirt.

Last we stopped at the fortune-teller wallah. His clever canary picked out some fortune cards from little boxes. Then he looked at Pushpa and said, "You will soon be getting married to a handsome, dark-haired boy!" (The man said this, not the canary.) I think this was very easy for the fortune-wallah. Well, we <u>were</u> carrying wedding things. And nearly <u>all</u> Indians have dark hair!

113

Walking around the streets here you are never being bored. You are being shouted at, pushed over and knocked flat on your bottoms! But you are <u>never</u> being bored! Arf arf!

I'll write to you soon.

Bye bye from,

Hari and his hurting feet

24 November

Dear chumji,

It is nearly time for Pushpa's wedding. It will be very, very BIG. There will be nearly <u>one hundred</u> guests. And they will <u>all</u> be starving hungry. Mamaji, Pushpa, Auntie Meena and their friends are cooking like crazy. Because there will be so many people to feed they are doing their cooking in great big pans! They are <u>enormous</u>! But Daada says they aren't nearly as big as the ones he once saw at the place called Dargah in Rajasthan. He says those ones were so big that after the feast was served and all eaten up, the people could get inside them and dance around!

While all this cooking is happening, Daddyji and me and Little Hari are feeling hungry non-stop. Because we can smell good food <u>all the time</u>. Penji, it is driving us up the bend!

I would like you to come to my sister's wedding and taste all the lovely food we will have. Do you eat curry? Well, here is a surprise for you. There is <u>NO</u> curry in India. Curry is just a word that people from other countries use to talk about most of our food in India. Now I will put you in the know about <u>real</u> Indian food. When you have read this, your stomach will be shouting to try some. One thing, though. There are thousands of different food things all over India. I would need a thousand letters for them all. Here is just a taste. So eat up!

RICES, SPICES...AND ALL THINGS NICES ~
by Number One Hari.

Breads ~ This is called roti, and the most common sort is chapatis. They are made from mixed up flour and water. You cook them on a tawa hot metal plate (a bit like a frying pan). If you are Hindu you put it this way:

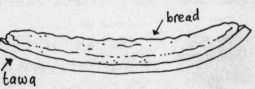

and if you are a Muslim this way:

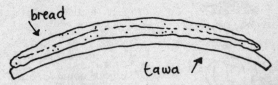

Handkerchief bread is a very big flappy chapati.

Do not blow your nose on it!

Rices ~ This is very important food all around India. More people eat it in the south than the north. My favourite sort of rice is called "basmati".

Spices ~ These are very important! I have just counted my mum's. She has got 25 (all different) on her shelfs! They add nice tastes to food and do good health things for your body and your head. Here are some and why they are good.

· Turmeric - it is yellow and kills germs inside and outside your body.

· Coriander - helps you go to the toilet if you are stuck up inside.

· Black pepper - gives good energy to ladies with a new baby.

· Garlic - good for getting your blood going around you.

· Chillies - Hot seed that came here with some Portuguese people. They got them from South America.

There are many more. A mix-up of spices is called a masala. This is what people from other places think is curry powder.

Meats ~ A lot of Indian people do not eat

meat because their religions say, "No . . . you musn't!" But some do - more in north India than south. Here is a nice meat thing called Tandoori chicken. (Maybe you know it?) After it is made dead the chicken is soaked in yoghurts, chillies and spices. Oh, and the feathers and beaks are taken off first. A tandoor is an oven made of clay and it is in a hole in the ground. When it is very hot the chicken is popped inside. After 15 minutes it comes out sizzling and delicious! Hmmm! Eat it with onions, radishes and naan bread, also baked in the tandoor.

Drinks ~ We drink chai. You call it

tea. The British Empire had the idea of growing a big amount of tea bushes here. They wanted to sell lots of tea to Indian people to make money for their pockets. So to

make them get the chai-drinking habit they gave away cups of tea at stalls in the street. They also gave Indian people the new idea of putting sugar and milk with tea - not just water like they had before. Now to make our tea we put the tea and sugar and water and milk all together in a big pot, then we give it a good long cooking. Is this how you do yours? We like it best with <u>lots</u> of sugar dollops. It's very freshing. Hmmm.

On the train stations and some other places you have your tea in little clay pots. You drink your chai then just smash your tea cup on the floor. It doesn't matter. There are plenty more. A boy is making them on his potty wheel near by.

Another thing we drink is lassi. This is a sort of yoghurt but very thin for drinking with ice in it. Water is also very important for drinking here. In the hot and dry Thar desert in the west people have to drink four litres in a day to stop themselves drying up. I also like to drink orange squish and Cokes.

Paan ~ In a lot of places in India you will see grown-ups chewing happily, then spitting red splashes all over the floors and

walls. Do not be afraid. It is <u>not</u> their blood they are spitting! They are munching paan. It is made from a leaf full with chopped nuts and red paste. It helps them with their indigestion and they love it. You can buy it from paan wallahs on the pavement.

HOW WE DO OUR EATING ~ Mostly we do not eat with forks and knives. Just the fingers. My grand-daddy says using fork and knife is like watching a movie with your eyes closed. Because

it is nice to scoop your food and have a feel of it as you eat. And touching will help you know if it's hot. So you will not burn your tongues! If you like you can break off some of your chapati pieces and scoop your food. Or roll your rice into a small ball and dip it in your sauce.

Many people do not eat from a table. They put a white cloth on the floor and sit on little stools to eat from it. The food is on a lathi which is a metal tray with spaces for each thing. Or maybe on a banana leaf.

Now, after all that I am absolutely scrumptious. I am going for my dinner.

Enjoy your dinners,

Hari Number One

8 December

Dear thingummiji,

How are you today? Here in Old Delhi it was Pushpa's wedding. It is <u>still</u> Pushpa's wedding! The celebrations are going like a horse on fire! But I have sneaked away to do your letter. It will be my last one to you! I am doing my writing on the rooftop. In the courtyard space just below me, fireworks and music are banging away fit to blast! Uncle Darshan is filming everyone with his new second-hand video camera

so we can enjoy the party all over again when it is all over. Now I will tell you about today. And then I will <u>go</u>. Forever! (. . .or maybe just forbit!)

VERY, VERY EARLY THIS MORNING ~ We were all dressed up very smart and waiting for Vishal and his family to arrive. All of a sudden there was music playing in the street. "They are coming! They are coming!" shrieked Little Hari, and we both ran to see. YES! YES! A wedding-music band and a procession of laughing people were coming down our lane. Hari and me raced to greet them. But . . . *NO NO!* They marched <u>straight past</u> our block. It was <u>someone else's</u> wedding! There are marryings all over the place in Delhi at this time of year, you know. It is the wedding season! Maybe there will be wedding-parade jams!

A BIT LATER — BUT STILL VERY EARLY ~ More music came in the air. So we looked out again. Han! (Yes!) This time it was Vishal's family and friends and <u>our</u> band coming down the lane.

The noise was deafening! To give them extra loudness all the instruments were joined to an electric charger-upper on a truck. And so were Vishal's friends! They had covered themselves with glowing fluorescent lighting tubes and pretty bulbs! So they were all lit up.

A MOMENT LATER ~ Vishal came around the corner on a big white horse! He was wearing a natty pink turban on his head. His friends were all laughing and throwing tinsel on him. He looked very, very happy!

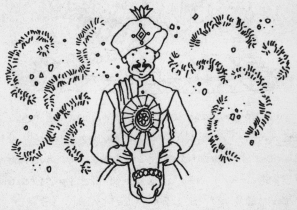

IN THE HOUSE ~ Pushpa and Vishal sat on the floor with the priest next to a fire in a tin box. All the relatives went past them and touched Pushpa's feet and put tilaks (another sort of spot, like a bindi) on Vishal's forehead. The priest said some special Hindu marrying words, then tied Vishal's scarf to Pushpa's shawl. After this they walked around the fire seven times (because they are going to stay married for <u>seven</u> of their lifetimes). Now they were properly married - so the feasting and fun could begin!

Now to my last and greatest piece of news. Next week I am starting at my <u>new school</u>. It is just near to us and is owned by the government. At first I will only go part of the time because I have still got to work to get money for our family. So there will be no time to write more letters to you.

But don't be sad old chumji! Things have turned out not too bad after all. We've had some laughs and fun. I've got some friends and a new school. <u>You've</u> got some new India knowledges (I hope!). My family have got a nice flat and some money. And Pushpa has got a husband!

Hmmmm? I wonder who Mum and Dad will choose for me to marry? Maybe another one of these kids of Uncle Darshan and Auntie Meena? I hope not!

Achaa! OK! I will get back to the eating and dancing now. Here is my last drawing for you. It is a cow I have been watching from up here on the roof. It is eating a flower garland that one of the wedding guests has dropped. I wonder if it will bring it luck? Or just the indigestions. (Arf arf!)

Ta Ta! Bye bye!

Hariji